PLOWING THE FIELDS DEVOTIONAL

A GUIDE TO PRAYING FOR THE LOST

FAITH COACH BOOKS
LEVELLAND, TEXAS

Copyright © 2012 David H. Rhoades

All rights reserved.

First Printing, *2012*
Second Printing, *2016*

ISBN: 0692636196
ISBN-13: 978-0692636190

Scripture quotations marked ESV are from The Holy Bible, English Standard Version® (ESV®), copyright © 2001 by Crossway, a publishing ministry of Good News Publishers. Used by permission. All rights reserved.

Scripture quotations marked HCSB are taken from the Holman Christian Standard Bible®, Copyright © 1999, 2000, 2002, 2003, 2009 by Holman Bible Publishers. Used by permission. Holman Christian Standard Bible®, Holman CSB®, and HCSB® are federally registered trademarks of Holman Bible Publishers.

Scripture quotations marked NASB are taken from the New American Standard Bible®, Copyright © 1960, 1962, 1963, 1968, 1971, 1972, 1973, 1975, 1977, 1995 by The Lockman Foundation. Used by permission. www.lockman.org

Scripture quotations marked NCV are taken from the New Century Version. Copyright © 2005 by Thomas Nelson, Inc. Used by permission. All rights reserved.

Scripture quotations marked NIV are taken from the Holy Bible, New International Version®, NIV®. Copyright © 1973, 1978, 1984, 2011 by Biblica, Inc.™ Used by permission of Zondervan. All rights reserved worldwide. www.zondervan.com. The "NIV" and "New International Version" are trademarks registered in the United States Patent and Trademark Office by Biblica, Inc.™

Scripture quotations marked NLT are taken from the Holy Bible, New Living Translation, copyright © 1996, 2004, 2007 by Tyndale House Foundation. Used by permission of Tyndale House Publishers, Inc., Carol Stream, Illinois 60188. All rights reserved.

Inspired by and dedicated to my grandparents
Winfred and Dean Bridwell
who effectively led hundreds of people to Christ
through their prayers, witness, and love.

ACKNOWLEDGEMENTS

In the back of the book, you will find just a few of the many written resources that have influenced my life and ministry. Just as inspirational are the intercessors whose ministries have personally touched my life—including Don Miller of Bible Based Ministries, Pastor Jimmy Draper, Jon Moore of the Jon Moore Evangelistic Association, and Kevin Meador of Kingdom Praying.

It is my prayer that the Lord may use this devotional to speak to your heart.

Introduction

Jesus told us to make disciples of the nations. This is the heartbeat of God.

When God's passion becomes ours, it will be reflected in our prayers. No longer will we be satisfied praying for selfish ends. We will intercede on behalf of others that they might be saved.

We can rest assured that God will move as we align ourselves with His will and pray accordingly. History is filled with mighty movements of God that began as His people prayed. May God move again in our midst.

This devotional is designed to help you gain a greater passion for praying for lost people. God is looking for those who will plow the fields through prayer as the Holy Spirit prepares the hearts of the lost to receive the gospel.

Throughout this devotional, you will be asked to pray for a lost loved one or friend by name. Perhaps there are many that you could list who need to receive Christ. With each day's devotion there is a page dedicated for your personal notes. Write out your own prayer or any other thought the Lord brings to your mind. Perhaps in the months and years to come, you can reflect on what God was doing in your heart at this time.

Day 1

Not to us, O Lord, not to us, but to your name give glory, for the sake of your steadfast love and your faithfulness! Why should the nations say, "Where is their God?" Our God is in the heavens; he does all that he pleases. Psalm 115:1-3 (ESV)

Everything we do—including praying for the lost—is to give God glory. When we allow ourselves to be compelled by other motivations, our hearts drift from God.

God is able to accomplish anything He desires. Think of a lost person whose heart is cold toward God—perhaps your spouse, child, grandchild, friend, co-worker, or schoolmate. Do you find yourself thinking that he or she is beyond God's reach? Although the situation can seem hopeless, consider the ability of God and be encouraged.

Prayer:

Creator of all, my faith in You is weak. Satan wants to discourage me from praying for the lost. But You are the Sovereign One, and I believe in You. For Your own glory's sake, bring salvation to my loved one. Amen.

My Notes:

Day 2

I urge that supplications, prayers, intercessions, and thanksgivings be made for all people, for kings and all who are in high positions, that we may lead a peaceful and quiet life, godly and dignified in every way. This is good, and it is pleasing in the sight of God our Savior, who desires all people to be saved and to come to the knowledge of the truth.

1 Timothy 2:1-4 (ESV)

Paul urged Timothy to compel the people of God to intercede on behalf of the lost. Even our prayers for the governing authorities is for the purpose of being able to live as effective witnesses of Christ.

As you pray, your compassion for lost people grows and your heart becomes aligned with God's heart. Your prayers are good and acceptable to Him, for He desires their salvation.

Prayer:

God our Savior, Your desires are pure and good. Help me to be more faithful in praying for my lost friend. Align my heart with Yours. Help me see people as You see them. Increase my compassion. Amen.

My Notes:

Day 3

The same Lord is the Lord of all and gives many blessings to all who trust in him, as the Scripture says, "Anyone who calls on the Lord will be saved." But before people can ask the Lord for help, they must believe in him; and before they can believe in him, they must hear about him; and for them to hear about the Lord, someone must tell them.

Romans 10:12-14 (NCV)

Some believe that the Lord only seeks the salvation of certain people, but this is not true. God is not ignoring your friend or hindering him from saving faith—just the opposite. The Lord is both willing and able to save your loved one.

So why hasn't your lost friend received Christ yet? Part of the answer rests in the fact that God has ordained salvation to be delivered to the lost through *our* efforts. He has entrusted us with the gospel. How can they hear unless someone tells them?

Prayer:

Heavenly Father, I don't want to be the reason my lost loved one has not heard the gospel. I want to be a faithful witness for You. Help me obey You in this. Teach me Your ways. Amen.

My Notes:

Day 4

Plant the good seeds of righteousness, and you will harvest a crop of love. Plow up the hard ground of your hearts, for now is the time to seek the Lord, that he may come and shower righteousness upon you.

Hosea 10:12 (NLT)

The most widely-used analogy in the Bible describing evangelism is that of a farmer. The farmer engages in three essential tasks: plowing the fields, planting the seed, and harvesting the produce. This is what is required of us.

Few believers are willing to engage in the first step of harvesting souls: plowing the soil of lost people's hearts. Prayer can break up the hardness both of your own heart and that of your loved one.

Prayer:

Seeker of my soul, You have called me to pray for the salvation of my loved one. I have heard Your call. Break the hardness of my heart and replace it with a heart transformed by Your Spirit. Prepare my friend's heart for the gospel. Amen.

My Notes:

Day 5

"As he was sowing, some seeds fell along the path, and the birds came and ate them up. Others fell on rocky ground, where there wasn't much soil, and they sprang up quickly since the soil wasn't deep. But when the sun came up they were scorched, and since they had no root, they withered. Others fell among thorns, and the thorns came up and choked them. Still others fell on good ground, and produced a crop: some 100, some 60, and some 30 times what was sown."

Matthew 13:4-8 (HCSB)

Are your efforts to share Christ fruitful? Do you produce a harvest? The sower's success or failure was not due to the seed, but to the soil. Perhaps the hard ground of your friend's heart still needs to be plowed through. God is able to break even the hardest of hearts to make it ready for the gospel, but He's waiting for you to intercede.

Prayer:

Lord of the harvest, you want me to bear fruit, but I need to sow seed on good ground. Tear out the obstacles that keep your seed from taking root. Cast the rocks from the heart of my lost friend. Cut off the thorns that choke out Your Word. Bring in Your harvest. Amen.

My Notes:

Day 6

Yes, truth is lacking; and he who turns aside from evil makes himself a prey. Now the Lord saw, and it was displeasing in His sight that there was no justice. And He saw that there was no man, and was astonished that there was no one to intercede.

Isaiah 59:15-16a (NASB)

The people of Israel were in a terrible situation. They had brought harm to themselves through their wickedness and unbelief. No one but God could deliver them.

Your lost loved one is in a similar situation. Lost people have an adversary—the devil—who has captured them. Only one Person can deliver them. Will you not intercede to Him on their behalf?

Prayer:

Mighty Deliverer, You are stronger than the adversary. All authority is in Your hands. Do the impossible by bringing salvation to the lost. Make those who are blind to the gospel see. Bring the spiritually dead to life. I believe in You. Amen.

My Notes:

Day 7

The effective prayer of a righteous man can accomplish much. Elijah was a man with a nature like ours, and he prayed earnestly that it would not rain, and it did not rain on the earth for three years and six months. Then he prayed again, and the sky poured rain and the earth produced its fruit. James 5:16-18 (NASB)

Could God have caused the rain to stop and then return without Elijah's prayers? Yes, but God chooses to move when we pray. Elijah was a righteous man, and he prayed in harmony with God's will.

It is God's desire to save your lost loved one. Will not your prayers move His heart to action? Or is there some unrighteousness in your life that hinders your fruitfulness? Cleanse your heart and intercede for your friend.

Prayer:

Giver of the rain, there is nothing outside Your control. You are intimately involved in every detail of my life. You know my heart. Cleanse me, Lord. Let Your showers of blessings flood the life of my lost friend. Amen.

My Notes:

Day 8

And the Lord's servant must not be quarrelsome but kind to everyone, able to teach, patiently enduring evil, correcting his opponents with gentleness. God may perhaps grant them repentance leading to a knowledge of the truth, and they may come to their senses and escape from the snare of the devil, after being captured by him to do his will.
2 Timothy 2:24-26 (ESV)

God is the Author of salvation, yet He has given us a role to play. As we live out our faith by being kind, teaching others, enduring evil, and remaining gentle, God enables the lost to repent.

These verses describe the spiritual condition of your lost loved one as being captured by the devil. Satan has imprisoned the lost, and they have no earthly chance of escape. Christ, however, has come to set the captives free.

Prayer:

Liberator of the captives, You can do all things. Grant repentance to my lost loved one. Lead my friend to the knowledge of the truth. Free the lost from the devil's grasp. Amen.

My Notes:

Day 9

"When a strong man, fully armed, guards his estate, his possessions are secure. But when one stronger than he attacks and overpowers him, he takes from him all his weapons he trusted in, and divides up his plunder."   Luke 11:21-22 (HCSB)

Jesus' critics accused Him of casting out demons with demonic power. He responded by sharing this brief analogy. The strong man is Satan, who desperately wants to keep his "possessions"—lost people.

Your lost loved one is currently in Satan's house and is carefully guarded by him. Have you given up hope of ever seeing your friend come to faith in Christ? Remember that Satan is no match for the Stronger Man—Jesus!

Prayer:

Lord Jesus, my hope needs to be renewed. My faith in You needs to be strengthened. Help me to pray as I ought for my lost loved one. Today I resolve to believe that You can save. I ask You to bind Satan and set the lost free. Let me see Your salvation. Amen.

My Notes:

Day 10

We know that we are of God, and the whole world is under the sway of the evil one.   1 John 5:19 (HCSB)

There are only two kinds of people in the world: those who are of God, and those who are under the devil's sway. We may not always be able to discern the difference, but God knows the heart.

This verse pictures the world as a powerless, sleeping baby being cradled in the arms of Satan. His intentions are evil, but lost people are incapable and even unwilling to escape the power of the evil one. Pray that Christ awakens the lost to the truth and frees your loved one from Satan's grasp.

Prayer

God over all, there is nothing I can do in my own strength. My efforts are not enough. Would You move on my behalf? Awaken the sleeping from their slumber! Do whatever it takes to save my friend. Amen.

My Notes:

Day 11

[Jesus said to some people who claimed to believe in Him], "Why do you not understand what I say? It is because you cannot bear to hear my word. You are of your father the devil, and your will is to do your father's desires." John 8:43-44 (ESV)

Religious or spiritual people can be lost. The words of Jesus to these pretending believers were both stinging and true. Lost people are children of the devil, no matter how religious they are.

It is difficult to consider, but your lost loved one currently belongs to Satan's family. Without God's help, your friend will never even be able to comprehend the good news of Jesus. Pray that God rescues your loved one and adopts him or her into His own family.

Prayer:

Father, increase Your family today! Draw my friend to Yourself. Let me be an instrument of Your kindness and a witness of Your grace. Amen.

My Notes:

Day 12

Yes, in the past you lived the way the world lives, following the ruler of the evil powers that are above the earth. That same spirit is now working in those who refuse to obey God.   Ephesians 2:2 (NCV)

The devil is active in the lives of the lost. He does whatever he can to keep people from believing in Jesus. Without Christ, people are empowered by Satan, even though most do not realize it. Satan tempts them to make self-destructive decisions. The more deeply caught in Satan's grasp, the more blinded they are to the gospel.

What is true of your lost friend was once true of you. Yet God saved you. What kind of barriers did God have to break through to get your attention? Do you believe God can do the same for the lost person for whom you are interceding?

Prayer:

Giver of the new birth, my friend lives like the world because he or she is of the world. Stop the work of Satan in the hearts of the lost. Awaken my friend to new life in Christ. Amen.

My Notes:

Day 13

If the Good News that we preach is hidden, it is hidden only to those who are lost. The devil who rules this world has blinded the minds of those who do not believe. They cannot see the light of the Good News—the Good News about the glory of Christ, who is exactly like God.

2 Corinthians 4:3-4 (NCV)

The only message that can transform a person's heart and change his eternity is the gospel of Jesus Christ. The gospel, however, is a truth that lost people cannot see or understand. Why? Because Satan and his false angels are constantly at work to keep people from hearing and understanding the good news of Jesus.

If only your lost loved one could see Christ clearly, he or she would run to Him and embrace Him in faith. Ask God to open the eyes of the lost to the gospel.

Prayer:

All-seeing Father, You know the heart of the one I love. Remove the demonic blinders that hinders my friend from seeing the gospel clearly. And remove anything in my life that distracts people from seeing Christ. Amen.

My Notes:

Day 14

"I am sending you to them to open their eyes so that they may turn away from darkness to the light, away from the power of Satan and to God. Then their sins can be forgiven, and they can have a place with those people who have been made holy by believing in Me."

Acts 26:17-18 (NCV)

Jesus personally gave Paul a very unique commission. He was to take the gospel to the Gentiles—people who were strangers to God and His ways. Without Jesus, the Gentiles would remain in darkness.

How can the blind see? How can the powerless overcome Satan? It can never happen unless God intervenes, and God moves when we pray. The salvation of your lost loved one may seem hopeless, but with God all things are possible. Jesus has come to give sight to the blind.

Prayer:

Mighty One of Israel, salvation is for Your glory, for only You can overcome the devil's power in the lives of the lost. Save my friend so Your glory may increase. Amen.

My Notes:

Day 15

If I regard wickedness in my heart, the Lord will not hear; but certainly God has heard; He has given heed to the voice of my prayer. Blessed be God, who has not turned away my prayer nor His lovingkindness from me. Psalm 66:18-20 (NASB)

After recounting how the Lord had tested Israel in Egypt and delivered them to the Promised Land, the psalmist responded to God with praise and sacrifice. His worship would have been meaningless if sin was in his heart.

Even though the Lord desires to save your loved one, your prayers will be hindered if you hold on to your sin. Consider the cost of disobedience and choose wisely how to live. What is hindering your walk with Christ? An immoral relationship? A secret sin? Anger and pride? Cut it out of your life. Seek the help of other godly believers.

Prayer:

Righteous One, I can overlook my sin no longer. Cleanse my heart and change my mind. Restore to me the joy of my salvation. Fill me with Your Spirit. May my life be aligned with Your will. Amen.

My Notes:

Day 16

"I am the vine; you are the branches. The one who remains in Me and I in him produces much fruit, because you can do nothing without Me. If anyone does not remain in Me, he is thrown aside like a branch and he withers. They gather them, throw them into the fire, and they are burned. If you remain in Me and My words remain in you, ask whatever you want and it will be done for you."

John 15:5-7 (HCSB)

When you are connected to the vine, you will produce fruit. The key to answered prayer is union with Jesus. When you are in close fellowship with Christ, His words will control your mind. Your prayers will then conform to the Father's desires. Because it is God's desire to save the lost, the results are certain.

Prayer:

God our Savior, I am still learning to remain in Christ. Help me identify those attitudes and actions that move me away from You. Teach me Your ways. Answer my prayers according to Your will. Amen.

My Notes:

Day 17

"By this my Father is glorified, that you bear much fruit and so prove to be my disciples." John 15:8 (ESV)

Why do you want to see your lost loved one be saved? Is it for your own sense of accomplishment, or perhaps out of pride for the family name? If you want God to answer your prayers, you motives must be right.

The glory of God must be your primary motive in praying for the lost. He will not bless selfish prayers, even if it is for a good end. In this verse, Jesus reminds us that not only do people know a tree by its fruit, but also that God is glorified when something He created fulfills its purpose.

Prayer:

God of all knowledge, I can hide nothing from You. You see the hidden motives of my heart even better than I can. Reveal my motives to me so I can be right with You. I want to bear fruit and accomplish the purpose You created me to fulfill. Amen.

My Notes:

Day 18

Let us not become weary in doing good, for at the proper time we will reap a harvest if we do not give up. Therefore, as we have opportunity, let us do good to all people, especially to those who belong to the family of believers. Galatians 6:9-10 (NIV)

The principles of the harvest are universal. We reap what we sow in our own spirit as well as our prayers.

One of Satan's tactics to make you ineffective in your walk with Christ is to discourage you. Perhaps difficulties have come into your life since you began praying for the lost. It may seem that the loved one you are praying for is growing farther away from God rather than closer to Him. Don't stop praying! There is a spiritual battle going on, and Satan will not give that person up without a fight.

Prayer:

Heavenly Father, I believe that I will reap what I sow. I pray that my own spirit will not become discouraged or distracted by the devil's tactics. Help keep my focus on Your truth, not Satan's lies. Amen.

My Notes:

Day 19

Then he said to me, "Fear not, Daniel, for from the first day that you set your heart to understand and humbled yourself before your God, your words have been heard, and I have come because of your words. The prince of the kingdom of Persia withstood me twenty-one days, but Michael, one of the chief princes, came to help me, for I was left there with the kings of Persia. Daniel 10:12-13 (ESV)

Daniel was interceding on behalf of Israel, but his answer from heaven was delayed by a satanic force. Daniel did not know why his prayers were not answered immediately, but he kept praying. Perhaps the answers to your prayers seem delayed, too. Keep praying for the lost to be saved, for God may be teaching you about perseverance, patience, or faith. Remember, your prayers have an influence in the spiritual struggles between the forces of God and the forces of the devil.

Prayer:

God of all power, I do not know what is happening in the spiritual realm, but I believe You are working. Teach me to persevere in my prayers. Strengthen my faith in You. Amen.

My Notes:

Day 20

And Jesus answered them, "Truly, I say to you, if you have faith and do not doubt, you will not only do what has been done to the fig tree, but even if you say to this mountain, 'Be taken up and thrown into the sea,' it will happen. And whatever you ask in prayer, you will receive if you have faith." Matthew 21:21-22 (ESV)

Jesus cursed the fig tree because it was a sign of hypocrisy, having leaves but no fruit. Then He answered the disciples' amazement by teaching them the importance of not doubting in prayer.

Do you doubt the Lord's ability or willingness to save your lost friend? Have faith in God as you intercede for your friend. The Lord can do all things, and He will accomplish His purposes.

Prayer:

Mover of the mountains, there is nothing too difficult for You. Strengthen my faith in You. Take away every doubt in my heart. I believe in You. Amen.

My Notes:

Day 21

Finally, be strong in the Lord and in the strength of his might. Put on the whole armor of God, that you may be able to stand against the schemes of the devil. Ephesians 6:10-11 (ESV)

In his final set of instructions to the church at Ephesus, Paul encouraged believers to find their strength in the Lord. Satan is constantly on the attack, but God has given us His armor. The full armor of God is truth, righteousness, peace, faith, salvation, and the Word of God. Wearing and utilizing God's armor is a powerful and sure defense.

As you intercede for the lost, remember also to pray for yourself. You lack nothing to win the battle. Avail yourself of God's provisions.

Prayer:

Mighty One, You are the Lord who supplies. You have given me everything I need for life and godliness. I put on Your armor today. I am ready to fight for the soul of my lost friend. Amen.

My Notes:

Day 22

They were astonished at His teaching because His message had authority.
Luke 4:32 (HCSB)

The message of Jesus is incredible because it does not rest upon the authority of religious experts or popular leaders. It stands as unique because it is truth in a world filled with lies. The words of Christ are the very words of God.

The words of Jesus resonate in everyone's heart because every person is made in the image of God. Humans are specially designed by God to receive His Word and have a relationship with Him. When the lost loved one for whom you are praying hears the words of Jesus, he or she is hearing eternal truth from God. Pray that your friend's heart is receptive. Pray also for the people who will be planting the seed of God's Word.

Prayer:

Righteous Teacher, Your Word is truth. Use it to dispel the darkness and false beliefs in my loved one's heart. I believe You can make the coldest of hearts alive to the gospel. Amen.

My Notes:

Day 23

They came and woke Him up, saying, "Master, Master, we're going to die!" Then He got up and rebuked the wind and the raging waves. So they ceased, and there was a calm. He said to them, "Where is your faith?" They were fearful and amazed, asking one another, "Who can this be? He commands even the winds and the waves, and they obey Him!" Luke 8:24-25 (HCSB)

If Jesus has authority over the physical forces of this world, does He not also have authority over spiritual forces? There are evil spiritual forces that hinder your lost friend from coming to faith in Christ. However, these satanic forces must obey Jesus. Believe in Jesus' authority, pray according to His will, and He will act.

Prayer:

Calmer of the storm, Your disciples' faith was strengthened when they witnessed the demonstration of Your power. Do the impossible again, Lord. Save my loved one who is far from you, and let this strengthen my faith. I believe in You. Amen.

My Notes:

Day 24

But Jesus rebuked him and said, "Be quiet and come out of him!" And throwing him down before them, the demon came out of him without hurting him at all. Amazement came over them all, and they kept saying to one another, "What is this message? For He commands the unclean spirits with authority and power, and they come out."

Luke 4:35-36 (HCSB)

In this episode of Jesus' ministry, there was a man in the synagogue who had the spirit of an unclean demon within him. When Jesus commanded the demonic force to leave, it had no choice but to obey.

Jesus has authority over all demonic powers, including those that hold your lost loved one captive. When was the last time you were awestruck by the work of God? Call upon Jesus to use His authority to free the lost.

Prayer:

Lord over all, even the darkest of forces must obey You. There are satanic forces working in the life of my friend. Exercise Your authority over these forces and cast them out. Bring salvation to my friend. Amen.

My Notes:

Day 25

"For this reason the Father loves me, because I lay down my life that I may take it up again. No one takes it from me, but I lay it down of my own accord. I have authority to lay it down, and I have authority to take it up again. This charge I have received from my Father."
John 10:17-18 (ESV)

From the beginning, our Heavenly Father has been forming a kingdom of believers to worship and serve Him freely. The death of Jesus on the cross was a necessary part of the plan to redeem us from our sin.

By His own authority Jesus willingly laid down His life so that God's purposes could be fulfilled. By His own authority Jesus rose from the grave so that we could have life. By His own authority Jesus can save your lost loved one.

Prayer:

Author of life, I pray that you save my lost friend today. I believe in Your authority, and I believe in Your power. My friend is spiritually dead. Quicken the heart and bring the captive into Your kingdom. Amen.

My Notes:

Day 26

"Which is easier, to say, 'Your sins have been forgiven you,' or to say, 'Get up and walk?' But, so that you may know that the Son of Man has authority on earth to forgive sins,"—He said to the paralytic—"I say to you, get up, and pick up your stretcher and go home." Immediately he got up before them, and picked up what he had been lying on, and went home glorifying God. Luke 5:23-25 (NASB)

The religious leaders thought Jesus was blaspheming God when He forgave the sins of the paralytic man. They did not realize that Jesus had authority to forgive sins, much less the authority to make a sick man whole.

The battle for souls is a battle that you can win. Why? Because Jesus has authority to forgive sins. Have faith in the Lord. He will hear your prayers.

Prayer:

Lord Jesus, I cannot save anyone from their sins, but You can! You have all authority and power. Accomplish what I cannot. I believe in You. Amen.

My Notes:

Day 27

"And I also say to you that you are Peter, and on this rock I will build My church, and the forces of Hades will not overpower it. I will give you the keys of the kingdom of heaven, and whatever you bind on earth is already bound in heaven, and whatever you loose on earth is already loosed in heaven." Matthew 16:18-19 (HCSB)

What precipitated this declaration of Jesus was a declaration by Peter himself: "You are the Christ, the Son of the living God." Jesus recognized Peter's faith and responded by teaching him an eternal truth about the power we have in Christ.

God has empowered His people to conquer the gates of hell. You have tremendous authority in Christ. Use it! Make the most of every opportunity to intercede on behalf of your lost friend.

Prayer:

Lord of hosts, all authority comes from You. You have empowered me to be involved in the battle for souls. I will pray. I will serve. I will go. Amen.

My Notes:

Day 28

He Himself is the propitiation for our sins; and not only for ours, but also for those of the whole world.   1 John 2:2 (HCSB)

Jesus died in our place to take away our sins. He became sin so that we would become the righteousness of God in Him. This truth is not reserved for us alone, but it can be received by anyone through faith in Christ.

There is no reason why anyone should go to hell. The only sin keeping people from God is the sin of unbelief. Jesus has already paid for the sins of the lost. His death is sufficient to cover all the sins committed in this history of the world. The devil, however, will not release the lost without a fight. If you want to see the salvation of your loved one, you must exercise the authority Christ has given you through prayer and evangelism.

Prayer:

Jesus my Lord, You have already paid the debt of sin. But Satan is holding my lost friend in his grasp. Overpower the evil one and bring freedom to the captive. Amen.

My Notes:

Day 29

For the weapons of our warfare are not of the flesh but have divine power to destroy strongholds. We destroy arguments and every lofty opinion raised against the knowledge of God, and take every thought captive to obey Christ.   2 Corinthians 10:4-5 (ESV)

The lost person's mind is the battlefield. Strongholds are ways of thinking that set a person's mind against God. If Satan has free access to continue influencing the mind of an unbeliever, he can keep the person from being saved. Do not think that your loved one will somehow be saved against his or her will. Instead, your task is to pray that God would free the mind of your friend from the blinding influences of Satan so he or she can see Christ clearly. Once a person's spiritual sight is clear, that person is then ready to receive Christ.

Prayer:

Lord God of heaven, strongholds are nothing for You. But to my lost friend, they are formidable. My loved one has been blinded by Satan's lies. Clear the dust from my friend's eyes to see Christ clearly. Amen.

My Notes:

Day 30

Then, looking at him, Jesus loved him and said to him, "You lack one thing: Go, sell all you have and give to the poor, and you will have treasure in heaven. Then come, follow Me." But he was stunned at this demand, and he went away grieving, because he had many possessions. Jesus looked around and said to His disciples, "How hard it is for those who have wealth to enter the kingdom of God."

Mark 10:21-23 (HCSB)

There was one stronghold keeping the rich young ruler from being saved: greed. His greed, however, simply disguised and guarded the only sin—unbelief—that kept him from receiving Christ.

What key stronghold do you believe keeps your loved one from receiving Christ? Lust? Bitterness? Addictions? Something else? Pray for its destruction so your friend will be free to see Christ and believe.

Prayer:

Dear Lord, I pray that the stronghold hindering my friend from believing in You will be torn down. May Your Spirit change unbelief to belief. Amen.

My Notes:

Day 31

Through His death He might destroy the one holding the power of death—that is, the Devil—and free those who were held in slavery all their lives by the fear of death. Hebrews 2:14-15 (HCSB)

Satan's one effective tool is deception. But God has provided you with powerful weapons that can overcome the ways in which the devil has deceived your loved one. The first weapon that we must consider is the blood of Christ. When we talk about the blood of Christ, we are referring to His death on the cross and the benefits we receive through it. Because of the cross, Satan's power has been nullified.

Plead the blood of Christ on behalf of your loved one. When you do, it serves as a reminder that the demonic forces influencing his or her life have been defeated. Satan must always answer to the authority of Jesus Christ.

Prayer:

Heavenly Father, Your Son's death paid the debt for all mankind. I plead the blood of Christ on behalf of my lost loved one. Set my friend free from Satan's deception today. Amen.

My Notes:

Day 32

"Lord, even the demons are subject to us in Your name!"
                                            Luke 10:17 (ESV)

In Luke 10, Jesus sent out seventy of His followers to go into towns and villages where He would soon venture. They were His emissaries, sharing the kingdom of God with those who were receptive. When they returned, they marveled at the authority they had.

The key to their success was that they did not do these things according to their own power, but in Jesus' name. The name of the Lord Jesus is a powerful weapon that can defeat the enemy. When you pray for your lost friend, you are engaging in the same battle as the seventy disciples: preparing people's hearts for His arrival.

Prayer:

Jesus, You are the Lord. You have destroyed the work of the evil one through your death. You have been seated at the right hand of the Father. No satanic force can withstand Your power. Destroy the strongholds keeping my lost friend from coming to You. Amen.

My Notes:

Day 33

Take...the sword of the Spirit, which is the word of God.
                                        Ephesians 6:17 (ESV)

Intercessors are those who consistently march forward—on the attack against demonic forces. We are invaders of a satanic kingdom. We are storming the gates of hell, where the lost are trapped. We must utilize the weapons God has given us. Of all the weapons listed in Ephesians 6, there is only one that can be used on offense as well as defense: the Word of God.

Take the time to learn how to pray God's Word, personalizing it as an appeal to God. When we pray the Bible on behalf of the lost, our prayers become incredibly effective. Why? Because the Bible is the Word of God Himself. We are praying in perfect unity with God's mind. God's Word is truth, and the Lord honors truthful prayers.

Prayer:

True One, honor Your Word. Let it not return void. Teach me to pray the Scriptures so my heart can be one with Yours. Amen.

My Notes:

Day 34

The moment they began their shouts and praises, the LORD set an ambush against the Ammonites, Moabites, and the inhabitants of Mount Seir who came to fight against Judah, and they were defeated.
                                              2 Chronicles 20:22 (HCSB)

In this passage, the people of Judah were in a battle against multiple enemies. They discovered that they did not have to fight the battle, but only position themselves to see the salvation of the Lord. Because they believed the Lord's promises, they began to praise Him even *before* the battle began.

Praise is a strong weapon that can win the battle against the enemy. Although it may seem like God is not working in the life of your lost friend, know that He is. Are you able to praise God for the work that He is yet to do?

Prayer:

Most glorious God, You inhabit my praise. I praise You for who You are. I thank You today for the work You are doing in my lost loved one. Your work will be accomplished in Your perfect timing. Amen.

My Notes:

Day 35

"Is not this the fast that I choose: to loose the bonds of wickedness, to undo the straps of the yoke, to let the oppressed go free, and to break every yoke?" Isaiah 58:6 (ESV)

In Isaiah's day, God's people were mistreating each other and then going through the rituals of worship, including fasting. The Lord is more concerned with how we treat one another than with the outward practices of worship. He will not honor our prayers if we are the cause of division among His people.

If you will do what you can to make your relationships with others right, fasting can be a powerful experience. Biblical fasting sets worldly things aside so you can focus on the presence of the Lord. As such, it honors God, who can defeat the enemy in the hearts of the lost.

Prayer:

Lord God, let my sole devotion be to You. Increase my love for You. I set aside the things of this world because I don't want anything to interfere with My relationship with You. Please answer my prayers and save my lost friend. Amen.

My Notes:

Day 36

Pray at all times in the Spirit with every prayer and request, and stay alert in this with all perseverance and intercession for all the saints. Pray also for me, that the message may be given to me when I open my mouth to make known with boldness the mystery of the gospel. For this I am an ambassador in chains. Pray that I might be bold enough in Him to speak as I should. Ephesians 6:18-20 (HCSB)

Even though Paul was in prison for the sake of the gospel, he knew the power of God could not be held captive. As we persevere in prayer for the saints, let us also continue to pray for the lost. Effective intercessors are persistent intercessors. Why is perseverance necessary as we pray for the salvation of the lost? It is not because we are trying to convince God to do something He doesn't want to do; rather, it is because the devil is reluctant to give them up.

Prayer:

Father, help me not give up too quickly in prayer. Teach me that the situation is never so bleak that I should stop praying. I will continue to intercede until the strong man is bound and strongholds come down. Amen.

My Notes:

Day 37

For we do not wrestle against flesh and blood, but against the rulers, against the authorities, against the cosmic powers over this present darkness, against the spiritual forces of evil in the heavenly places. Therefore take up the whole armor of God, that you may be able to withstand in the evil day, and having done all, to stand firm.

Ephesians 6:12-13 (ESV)

Lost people are not the enemy. They are friends who have been captured by the enemy. Many times they will say or do things that mimic the thoughts of the one who has ensnared them. Do not become angry at them, for their words and actions are reminders to us that the battle is ongoing.

Because you are indeed in a spiritual battle for souls, you need to be sober and aggressive. The devil is playing for keeps. He seeks to steal, kill, and destroy. Take up God's armor and be engaged in the battle.

Prayer:

Lord God, You have made me more than a conqueror. I lift up Your name in praise. May You receive glory both in my life and the life of my lost friend. Amen.

My Notes:

Day 38

When the apostles who were still in Jerusalem heard that the people of Samaria had accepted the word of God, they sent Peter and John to them. When Peter and John arrived, they prayed that the Samaritan believers might receive the Holy Spirit. Acts 8:14-15 (NCV)

God places great value on the unity of His people. Notice that Peter and John prayed together for the Samaritan believers. When they did, God fulfilled His plan in the Samaritans.

Are you humble and desperate enough to ask other Christians to join you in prayer for your lost loved one? If you are too ashamed to pray with other believers for the lost, your pride may hinder your prayers and enable demonic forces to maintain a stronghold in your friend.

Prayer:

Father of lights, don't allow my pride to hinder me from asking for another believer's help in prayer. I humble myself before You today. Lead me to share with another intercessor my desire to see my friend saved. Amen.

My Notes:

Day 39

"Present your case," the LORD says. "Bring forward your strong arguments," the King of Jacob says.   Isaiah 41:21 (NASB)

In this passage, the Lord challenges unbelievers to prove the reality and power of their idols. Their case has no merit because it is built upon lies.

When you, however, come before the Lord in prayer, you can plead your case with confidence. How do you do this? Simply by giving God biblical reasons to answer your prayer. The Lord wants you to make your best case before Him to ensure that your heart is aligned with His. When your heart reflects God's heart, you can ask whatever you want and He will grant it.

Prayer:

King of Jacob, I want what You already desire: the salvation of the lost. Teach me to put my best case forward when I come to You in prayer. Let my words reflect Your heart. Amen.

My Notes:

Day 40

Deeply hurt, Hannah prayed to the LORD and wept with many tears.
1 Samuel 1:10 (HCSB)

More than anything, Hannah wanted to have a son. She agonized in prayer, knowing that this was something that only the Lord could do.

Like Hannah, you are an intercessor who may agonize in prayer. While her prayer was for a son, yours is for a lost loved one. The Lord is the only hope to rectify the situation. When the Spirit of God burdens your heart over the lost to the point where you weep in prayer, continue to pray! Just as in Hannah's situation, God may be birthing something new.

Prayer:

Comforter, it hurts me to consider the condition of my loved one. I am frightened when I think about the destiny of those who do not believe in Jesus. Do whatever it takes to save my friend. Grant new birth to the lost. Amen.

My Notes:

Day 41

I am speaking the truth in Christ—I am not lying; my conscience bears me witness in the Holy Spirit—that I have great sorrow and unceasing anguish in my heart. For I could wish that I myself were accursed and cut off from Christ for the sake of my brothers, my kinsmen according to the flesh. Romans 9:1-3 (ESV)

The apostle Paul was a Jew, and it broke his heart that so many of his kinsmen rejected their own Messiah. Paul was willing to trade places with them if only they would receive the Lord Jesus. God would never allow us to go to hell in the place of another person, but that is how desperately Paul desired to see the salvation of people he loved.

Are you willing to pray, "Lord, do whatever it takes to save my lost loved one!"? What would you sacrifice to see your friend saved?

Prayer:

Lord Jesus, You made the ultimate sacrifice to save us. Help me to have a sacrificial spirit. Do whatever it takes to save my friend. I cry out to You in desperation. Amen.

My Notes:

Day 42

Those who sow in tears shall reap with shouts of joy! He who goes out weeping, bearing the seed for sowing, shall come home with shouts of joy, bringing his sheaves with him. Psalm 126:5-6 (ESV)

This psalm was written after God's people returned from being exiled in Babylon. Those who once were captives now were set free. These believers understood what it meant to sow tears and reap joy.

Let this same principle of sowing and reaping be an encouragement to you as you seek the salvation of your lost loved one. Does your friend's spiritual condition bring you to tears? Many times a harvest does not come without heartbreak.

Prayer:

Spirit of God, my heart is broken because my friend is without Christ. The burden I carry is heavy. Hear the cry of my heart, and do a work that only You can do. Turn my tears into a harvest. Amen.

My Notes:

Day 43

From the beginning God has chosen you for salvation through sanctification by the Spirit and through belief in the truth. He called you to this through our gospel, so that you might obtain the glory of our Lord Jesus Christ.   2 Thessalonians 2:13-14 (HCSB)

According to these verses, God has ordained that salvation occur through two interconnected realities: the Holy Spirit's ministry of setting people apart and people's belief in Christ. How the divine and human intersect in the heart of man is a great mystery. But we know that through prayer we have a role to play in this process.

As you intercede for your lost loved one, agree with God about his or her sanctification. Pray that your friend will believe in the truth about Christ and partake in the glory of Him.

Prayer:

Holy One, set apart my loved one for salvation. Sanctify my friend by Your Spirit and through belief in the truth. Fulfill Your work in the life of the lost. Amen.

My Notes:

Day 44

Do you think lightly of the riches of His kindness and tolerance and patience, not knowing that the kindness of God leads you to repentance?
Romans 2:4 (NASB)

In this passage, Paul is rebuking those who commit evil acts and then judge others for doing the same. As believers, we should remember that our salvation only occurred because of God's goodness. Scripture warns us that God's kindness should not be taken for granted, but rather inspire us to a repentant life.

How will repentance occur in the heart of the lost? Repentance can happen as your loved one experiences God's goodness and interprets it as being an expression of love. Pray that your friend would experience blessings and come to a new understanding of God's nature.

Prayer:

Loving Father, bless my lost loved one today. May Your love, kindness, and goodness overflow from my heart even when difficulties arise. Amen.

My Notes:

Day 45

"And when he comes, he will convict the world concerning sin and righteousness and judgment: concerning sin, because they do not believe in me." John 16:8-9 (ESV)

In the evening before His arrest and crucifixion, Jesus instructed His disciples that He would leave and the Holy Spirit would come in His place. One of the ministries of the Holy Spirit would be to bring conviction to unbelieving hearts.

It is the Holy Spirit's job—not yours—to convict the lost of the sin of unbelief. Take care that your words are prompted by the Spirit. Allow the Holy Spirit to do His work through you. Your task is to pray, live a Spirit-driven life, and share the gospel. As you intercede, ask the Holy Spirit to accomplish this work of conviction in your lost friend's life.

Prayer:

Holy Spirit, You know the heart of my lost loved one. My friend does not yet believe in Christ. Accomplish Your work of conviction. Pierce my friend's heart. Amen.

My Notes:

Day 46

For God, who said, "Let light shine out of darkness," has shone in our hearts to give the light of the knowledge of the glory of God in the face of Jesus Christ.   2 Corinthians 4:6 (ESV)

God created light out of darkness by speaking it into existence. Paul recalls this act of creation and sees a spiritual parallel in the hearts of believers: God shines in our hearts to reflect His glory.

When God is glorified through you, He illuminates the blinded minds of those without Christ. Once your lost friend's mind is illuminated, God can use you to explain the gospel to him. Pray that God will give sight to those whose minds are blinded to the gospel.

Prayer:

Light of the world, only You can cause the blind to see. Remove from my heart anything that might block the light of Your glory from shining through. Let people see Christ in me. Amen.

My Notes:

Day 47

When he saw the crowds, he had compassion for them, because they were harassed and helpless, like sheep without a shepherd. Then he said to his disciples, "The harvest is plentiful, but the laborers are few; therefore, pray earnestly to the Lord of the harvest to send out laborers into His harvest." Matthew 9:36-38 (ESV)

The more you become like Christ, the more you will see people as He does. As you intercede for your lost loved one, it is also beneficial to pray for the believer whom God will send to be a witness. There cannot be a harvest without workers to bring it in. Pray for more Christians to become true laborers for the harvest. Ask God to send someone to share the gospel with your lost friend.

Prayer:

Lord of the harvest, equip Your people with the tools that will make them effective witnesses. Send someone to my loved one who needs the Lord Jesus. Here am I. Send me. Amen.

My Notes:

Day 48

"And now, Lord, consider their threats, and grant that Your slaves may speak Your message with complete boldness, while You stretch out Your hand for healing, signs, and wonders to be performed through the name of Your holy Servant Jesus." When they had prayed, the place where they were assembled was shaken, and they were all filled with the Holy Spirit and began to speak God's message with boldness.

Acts 4:29-31 (HCSB)

The disciples who voiced this prayer were in danger. The enemies of Christ threatened them with bodily punishment if they continued to tell people about Jesus. The disciples, however, did not pray for protection, but for boldness to continue witnessing.

Are you scared of being a witness? Even the most experienced witnesses for Christ can become nervous. Rest assured in the abilities of your Savior, and pray for boldness!

Prayer:

Master, You have created all things, and You have created Me to give you glory. Give me boldness as I witness for Christ. Amen.

My Notes:

Day 49

"For as the rain and the snow come down from heaven and do not return there but water the earth, making it bring forth and sprout, giving seed to the sower and bread to the eater, so shall my word be that goes out from my mouth; it shall not return to me empty, but it shall accomplish that which I purpose, and shall succeed in the thing for which I sent it." Isaiah 55:10-11 (ESV)

God has created everything for a purpose beyond itself. The rain and snow exists for the sake of making the earth fruitful. Likewise, God's Word bears fruit in the hearts of receptive people.

God's Word is powerful because God is powerful. His Word has never failed and it never will. As you pray for God's Word to be effective in the heart of your lost loved one, you have a promise from God Himself that He will do it.

Prayer:

Lord my Righteousness, You always tell the truth. You always carry out Your Word. You never fail. Accomplish Your will in my friend's life. Amen.

My Notes:

Day 50

"When I shut up the heavens so that there is no rain, or command the locust to devour the land, or send pestilence among my people, if my people who are called by my name humble themselves, and pray and seek my face and turn from their wicked ways, then I will hear from heaven and will forgive their sin and heal their land."

2 Chronicles 7:13-14 (ESV)

Previously Solomon had prayed that God would bless His people if they repented. Here, the Lord responds in the affirmative: He will hear His people's prayers and bless them if they turn from their sin and seek His face.

Only God can save your lost friend. Only He can bring revival to your heart, home, church, and nation.

Prayer:

Father, Son, and Spirit, You brought Your people out of Egypt. You sustained them in the wilderness. You defeated their enemies. You accomplished Your purposes of salvation in Christ. How can I stand in Your way? I humble myself before You. I seek Your face. I turn from my wickedness. Hear my cry. Forgive my sin. Bring in Your harvest. Amen.

My Notes:

Helpful Resources

Alone with God by John MacArthur

And the Place Was Shaken: How to Lead a Powerful Prayer Meeting by John Franklin

Bible-Based Praying: A Workbook on Prayer for People to Spend Time with God by Don Miller

Don't Just Stand There, Pray Something by Ron Dunn

Handbook to Prayer: Praying Scripture Back to God by Kenneth Boa

Liberating the Leader's Prayer Life by Terry Muck

The Necessity of Prayer by E. M. Bounds

The Possibilities of Prayer by E. M. Bounds

Power Through Prayer by E. M. Bounds

Praying Effectively for the Lost by Lee Thomas

Praying in the Word of God by Kathleen Grant

Returning to Holiness: A Personal and Church-wide Journey to Revival by Greg Frizzell

The Weapon of Prayer by E. M. Bounds

Your Personal Guide to Fasting and Prayer by Bill Bright

www.ingramcontent.com/pod-product-compliance
Lightning Source LLC
Chambersburg PA
CBHW070524030426
42337CB00016B/2088